TOO LITTLE RANCH

CAROL CHAMPNEY

DEDICATION

Written for my beautiful grandchildren,
Anne-Marie Jean Thomas
Therese Claire Thomas
Natalie Catherine Thomas
Justin Paul Thomas
Cara Faith Curts
Kinsey June Curts

And,
My two beautiful daughters,
Monica Jean Thomas
Michelle Eileen Curts

ACKNOWLEDGMENTS

Cheryl Weller, if it weren't for you asking me to teach Becky and Julie piano, I probably would have never considered teaching. It was definitely not on my radar. God has interesting ways of bringing about His plan for our lives. Thank you from the bottom of my heart for being a part of His plan for my life.

To my husband, Roger, thank you for standing by me when I stopped working at the fire department to stay home with our girls. Your love and support have been constant. I am so blessed by your steadfast commitment to me. I love you honey bun.

Many thanks to all the piano students I've had the privilege of teaching. You have given me years of joy, entertainment, fun, pleasure, and great satisfaction watching you grow up and learn to play the piano.

To my piano parents, I commend you and humbly thank you. You gave your children one of the best gifts you could give---the gift of music.

Sarah Kurpius, it was during your tumultuous Jr. High years that this lesson and story were born. Remember "the intervention lesson?"

Grace Newcomb, my illustrator, thank you for buying a computer program specifically for pencil sketch drawings to complete this project. You were 15 years old when you drew these for me. I know, it's been about 5 years ago! Sometimes life takes a different turn, and indeed that is what happened after I started writing this book. Thank you, Grace. I love your artwork!

Debbie Bledsoe, I couldn't have completed this book without your encouragement and editing expertise. When my eyes were blurry from writing, you came to my rescue and offered suggestions to complete my thoughts. Editing is no small task, and I am so grateful for you standing beside me to "git 'er done!"

TABLE OF CONTENTS

Grace Newcomb

CHAPTER ONE

"BY JOVE! I THINK YOU'VE GOT IT!"

"By Jove! I think you've got it!" Mrs. C exclaimed with a British accent. Her piano students thought it was the funniest thing ever when she spoke with an accent! Secretly, they also thought she was a *little weird*!

After hearing it more times than he could remember, one of her students finally asked her, "Mrs. C, why do you always say that with a funny accent?" She smiled and looked off in the distance as if she had imagined something.

In her very best British accent, Mrs. C replied, "Oh, Josh, because I like pretending I'm a famous actress on a *large* stage, in front of a *very* large audience." Eyes now closed, she paused a moment glowing in the thought of her dream actually being real. As she opened her eyes, her imaginary audience disappeared, and all she saw was Josh staring at her.

"Ahhh, but alas, Josh, *you* are my only audience right now. My audience of one." Coming back to her senses and speaking in her usual voice, she smiled and said, "Besides, it makes you laugh!" Josh did laugh as he secretly thought, "Wow, she really *is* weird!"

Pointing to the music, bringing Josh's attention back to his piano lesson, Mrs. C said, "Now, let's hear you play measure twelve again. Play it *juuust* the way you played it before."

Josh played measure twelve once again. "That was marvelous! Simply *maaaarvelous*!

CHAPTER TWO

WHO IS MRS. C?

Who is "Mrs. C?" It's *me*! Grandma Carol! Did you know that when Monica and Michelle were growing up, I taught piano lessons? I never planned to teach piano lessons. It wasn't until my friend, Mrs. Weller, asked if I would teach her daughters to play. I said I would, and that's how I started teaching piano lessons.

Music has always been a big part of my life. For as long as I can remember, Great Grandma Jean would turn on the TV every Saturday night so we could watch the Lawrence Welk Show. It was a musical variety show. Lawrence Welk conducted a live orchestra. Besides the orchestra, the cast included ballroom dancers, tap dancers, piano players, accordion players, and many singers.

Sunday nights, we watched the Ed Sullivan Show. His guest performers were different each week. There were classical musicians, opera singers, famous recording artists, songwriters, comedians, ballet dancers, and even circus performers.

One of my favorite parts of the show was when Ed Sullivan talked to the famous Italian mouse puppet, Topo Gigio. It's pronounced "toe-poe **jee**-joe." He greeted Ed Sullivan with, "Hello, Eddie!" Topo Gigio ended his weekly visits by singing in a soft low voice "Eddie, kiss me good night!" (Pronounced as "Keesa me goo'night!").

I watched both those shows for 20 years. I loved the music and dancers, but what I loved most were the singers. Watching these shows gave me a love of music, entertainment, and performing. When I was seven years old I decided I wanted to be an actress and a singer.

My favorite singer is Reba McEntire. She is a country-western singer and is just a couple years older than I am.

There are many reasons why I like Reba McEntire. First, I like the way she can tell a story when she sings.

Reba has curly, red hair. I, too, have curly red hair.

Reba sang the National Anthem at rodeos. I've always wanted to sing the National Anthem at rodeos, too!

Reba has her very own horse. I didn't have a horse as a child, but I always wanted one.

Reba and her horse competed in barrel racing at rodeos. My family went to rodeos, too. I loved to watch the barrel racers because they were usually girls who wore pretty cowgirl outfits. I also wanted to be a barrel racer.

Reba is also an actress. She has performed on Broadway in New York. I have been in plays too. But only in Washington.

Reba starred in her own TV show. Guess what? I wanted to be on TV too!

As you can see, Miss Reba and I have a lot in common. But, she is famous, and I am not!

I have lots of other interests, too. I enjoy learning different languages, like French and Spanish. I like taking pictures of old barns. I enjoy going to see live entertainment. I like sewing, crocheting, knitting, tie-dying tee shirts, baking cinnamon rolls, bread, and cookies. (I like to eat the cookie dough more than I like the baked cookies!) I love to write. Oh my goodness, so many things! Did I mention I love animals?

I bet you already know I love dogs. But did you know I like lots of other animals, too?

Grace Newcomb

CHAPTER THREE

THE LITTLE BLACK PUPPY

Before Monica and Michelle were born, Grandpa Roger and I bought his Grandpa's house in Tacoma, Washington. Grandpa Paul had recently passed away. When we bought the house, we also got Grandpa Paul's little white dog BJ. He was part poodle, short, and *very* overweight because Grandpa Paul fed him too many treats!

After BJ passed away, it was very quiet in our house. We missed having a dog. Grandpa and I went to the Humane Society and adopted a little white dog. He had a long body with short legs. We think he was part terrier. Grandpa named him Bootsy because he loved jumping headfirst into Grandpa's stinky work boots. Peeee-yewwww! Can you imagine seeing a little white puppy with its head buried inside a boot and his wagging tail sticking straight up in the air? It was a funny sight indeed! For four more years, it was just Grandpa, me, and Bootsy.

In 1985, Grandma and Grandpa moved from Tacoma to Puyallup, Washington. This is where we raised Monica and Michelle, along with a *few* animals.

When the girls were 4 and 5 years old, I told Grandpa, "Bootsy is *our* dog. I think it's time the girls had their very own dog that will grow up with them." Grandpa agreed. I had a black Labrador retriever named Puddles when I was little. He was such a good dog that I wanted Monica and Michelle to have a black Lab too. Lab is short for Labrador.

I know it's hard to believe, but this was before computers were in everyone's home. Telephones hung on the wall, usually in the kitchen. There were no cell phones or internet. If you wanted to buy or sell something, you placed an advertisement in the local newspaper's classified section. There was a specific column of the classifieds titled "Animals for Sale," and that's exactly where Grandpa Roger found the ad "Labrador puppies for sale."

Grandpa called the phone number listed in the ad. Yes, they still had puppies, and yes, we could come over that day.

Back in those days, Grandpa Roger often stopped at 7-ll stores to buy a "Big Gulp" soda pop and a package of Hostess doughnuts. As usual, Grandpa stopped at a 7-ll on our way to look at the puppies. The girls and I waited in the car while Grandpa bought his goodies. When he got back in the car, he surprised Monica and Michelle by tossing them a package of jelly beans. With soda pop, doughnuts, and jelly beans in hand, we drove to the address the man on the phone had given Grandpa.

As we pulled into the driveway, a nice gentleman greeted us. "Are you here to look at the puppies?"

"Yes we are," Grandpa Roger replied.

"Right this way," the gentleman said, waving his arm for us to follow him.

We excitedly followed him around to the side of his house. There, in a large dog kennel, were ten black Labrador puppies! When they saw us, they all started jumping up on the side of the kennel. I think they were just as excited to see us as we were to see them! It was hard to choose just one because all of them were black, and all ten of them were jumping. They looked like a bag of jumping black jellybeans!

Grandpa Roger finally said, "Let's take a look at that one." The gentleman opened the kennel gate and picked up the one that Grandpa had pointed out.

"This one has the biggest paws of the whole litter," said the gentleman as he set the puppy down on the ground. The puppy's tail was wagging so fast, you could tell he was happy and excited to be playing with us. It didn't take long for us to decide that this was the puppy we would take home.

The chubby little puppy rode in the back seat with the girls. As they resumed eating jelly beans, I asked, "What should we name him? He's black. Should we call him Blacky?" No, that name was too plain for such a cute puppy. We thought of a few other names, but none of them sounded good to us. Then, popping a black jelly bean into her mouth, Michelle exclaimed, "How about Jelly Bean?" We all laughed and immediately agreed his name would be Jelly Bean.

Along with owning an animal comes responsibility. The girls had to take turns feeding him, making sure he had water, and cleaning up his poop in the backyard! To be honest, I ended up feeding him most of the time, and Monica cleaned up the poop!

Jelly Bean lived a good long life of 13 years! Bootsy lived a much shorter life. After Bootsy died, Grandpa Roger missed having a little white dog.

CHAPTER FOUR

THE SURPRISE

I f there's one thing Grandpa Roger doesn't like, it's getting surprised. He gets great enjoyment out of planning things. So when someone surprises him, he's missed out on the fun of planning. Even so, I have surprised him a few times. But, unfortunately, it never turned out well.

When the girls were in elementary school, Grandpa often took them out to dinner and then to the shopping mall. It was their special time together.

He liked to sit on a bench in the mall and watch people. He would say, "I wonder what will be the weirdest thing we'll see tonight?" Another thing he liked to do at the mall was throwing a penny on the floor to see how far it rolled before it stopped. Silly Grandpa!

One November night, when Monica was ten years old and Michelle was nine, we all went to the mall to shop for

Christmas gifts. Michelle and I went in our car, and Monica and Grandpa went in his truck.

Michelle and I wandered through the mall, trying to get ideas of what to buy for Christmas presents. Wee didn't find anything we wanted to buy, so just for fun, we went into one of our favorite stores; the pet store.

Pet stores sell different kinds of small animals and all the supplies you need to take care of them. Goldfish, parakeets, guinea pigs, gerbils, turtles, kittens, and puppies are usually available. Oh, dear. This is a very tempting store for Michelle and me.

As Michelle and I walked through the entrance to the store, guess what we saw? Not goldfish. Not guinea pigs. Not gerbils. Not parakeets. Not kittens. But what we did see was the smallest, fluffiest, cutest little *white* puppies we had ever seen!

Of course, I asked the store clerk to open the crate so we could hold one. The puppy was so small he fit in the palm of *one* hand! Michelle and I each took turns holding him. Michelle wanted to take him home. I did too, but I knew Grandpa Roger would not be happy if I did, so I firmly said, "NO," and gave the puppy back to the clerk.

We continued walking around the store. Michelle kept hounding me to buy the puppy. "No, Dad would not be happy if we brought a puppy home."

"Yeah, but Dad *really* wants another *white* dog." Michelle begged.

"Yes, I know, but Dad does not like surprises," I said, trying to remain firm.

"But he'd *like* this one! He's been looking for a little white dog, Mom. Pleeeeeeeeeease can we get him?"

"No, Michelle." My determination to leave the puppy at the pet store was weakening. He was so soft and cute!

Michelle continued to think of reasons why we should buy the puppy. "It could be an early Christmas present!"

"No Michelle. Now come on, let's go." I said, trying to get out of the store before I gave in and bought the pup.

"Can I hold him just one more time?" she asked.

"Ohhh, alright." I should have said "NO" and immediately walked out of the store. The clerk handed the puppy to Michelle.

Without saying a word, Michelle cuddled him and looked at me with those puppy-dog eyes. You know, it's the way you look at your Mom when you really, *really* want something, and you are hoping she'll change her mind. I turned my head away, thinking it would help me resist.

The store was about to close. I urged Michelle to give the puppy back to the clerk. She held on to the white fluff ball and said very stubbornly, "I'm *not* going home without him!"

That was it. I gave in. "Alright, let's take him home and surprise Dad! It can be his early Christmas present!"

Oh boy. That was NOT the right thing to do. When you know you shouldn't do something, but you do it anyway, that's called sin. I sinned. I knew better, too. I had an awful feeling in the pit of my stomach. Grandpa Roger was going to be very upset with me.

Grandpa and Monica got home first. Quietly and very nervously, Michelle and I walked into the house. We called for Monica so we could show her the puppy before we gave it to Grandpa. He was in the family room watching TV. I said, "Hi honey, we have something for you. Close your eyes and hold out your hands." When his eyes were closed, I placed the little white fluff ball into his hands and said, "Okay, open your eyes! Surprise!"

Grandpa Roger could not believe his eyes. He did not smile, nor did he speak a word. All he did was look at me very angrily. My stomach felt terrible. I knew I shouldn't have bought the puppy. But what was I to do now? The mall was closed. I couldn't return him!

Trying to make the best of my poor decision, I said, "It's an early Christmas present honey." Grandpa was not impressed.

He was upset that I surprised him by bringing a puppy home. Even so, Grandpa agreed to keep him.

"It's your dog, Dad. What are you going to name him?" the girls asked. After thinking a while, Grandpa chose his own initials, RT for Roger Thomas. So that's what we called the little white fluff ball, RT.

Grandpa Roger told me,

"No More Animals!"

I told Grandpa I was sorry for buying the puppy when I knew I shouldn't have. I asked him to forgive me, and he did. I asked God to forgive me, too.

Even when we sin, Jesus loves us. He doesn't love what we've done, but He still loves us. The Bible says,

If we confess our sins, he is faithful and just to forgive our sins and cleanse us from all unrighteousness. ***I John 1:9***

I asked God to forgive me for sinning. I told him I was sorry for buying the puppy when I knew Grandpa would not want me to. I thanked God for forgiving me.

CHAPTER FIVE

"HERE KITTY, KITTY"

Cats. Cats. Lots of cats!

All ranches must have cats. Cats keep the mice away.

Before Monica and Michelle were born, I worked at a company that sold lumber. One late afternoon the company truck driver came into the office carrying a scared tiny kitten. He told us that while waiting for his truck to be loaded, he kept hearing a "Meow." He followed the sound, which led him to a dumpster. "Meow, meow." He lifted the lid of the dumpster and saw a kitten sitting on top of all the trash. He reached in and picked her up. She was so small that she fit into his shirt pocket.

"What are you going to do with that poor little kitty," I asked. "Find her a home," the truck driver replied. Before anyone else in the office could get their mouth open, I shouted, "I'll take her!"

Grandpa and I had just moved to Too Little Ranch, and we needed a farm cat. We named her Mama Kitty because through the years she had so many litters of kittens.

Remember when I told Grandpa Roger that the girls needed their own dog? Well, the same went for cats. We had Mama Kitty before they were born. I wanted them to have their own cats.

It just so happened that when the girls were in first and second grade, Michelle came home from school and said, "Mom! Kendra's cat had kittens!" Of course, I said we could go *look*. And, of course, we came home with two new kittens. Michelle fell in love with the black kitten named Matthew. Monica decided she wanted Matthew's sister, who was black and white. The pattern of her markings was very similar to those of a black and white cow. Monica considered naming her Cow Cat but finally settled on the name Checkers.

I take full responsibility for bringing home the next cat! But, I will say, Michelle went with me and picked him out. One of my piano students came for her lesson and announced that her cat had kittens. Well, you know what that means! That evening Michelle and I drove to the student's house and chose our Slinky---the Tabby cat. I think he was the best cat we ever had. He lived the longest, too.

You know the toy called a Slinky? That's precisely why I named him Slinky. As he walked across the yard, he would stretch his front legs waaaaay out as far as he could. Then he would gather his back legs up to meet his front legs. He did this over and over until he made his way across the backyard to the barn.

By the time we added more cats to our family, Monica and Michelle were teenagers. I don't quite remember how Michelle (yes, Michelle, again!) found out about our next cat. At any rate, she drove an hour one way to pick up Timmy, the Calico cat. He was already a barn cat and was used to living outside. Maybe that's why he was so feisty. We named him Timmy, after a boy we knew at church who was very rambunctious. That was the perfect name for him! Not only was he feisty, but he liked roaming the neighborhood, too. The only problem with that was the traffic. Unfortunately, he did not live very long.

As for Nigel and Itty Bitty---Michelle (yes, Michelle again!) was working at a drive-through coffee stand when a customer drove up to the window and showed her a litter of 6-week old kittens.

Uh-oh, you know what's coming next don't, you? She called me from work to tell me how cute these kittens were and then asked if she could bring one home. She described their coloring. "They aren't Siamese are they," I questioned. The reason I asked that is because Siamese cats are known for their loud meowing. It can get very annoying. And, they meow a lot!

"No, I'm not sure what kind they are." Okay, as long as they aren't Siamese, you might as well bring two home. We can't have just *one* kitten. Pick one out for me!"

At the time, I thought, "Oh dear. What are we going to tell Grandpa Roger?" The kittens were only 6 weeks old--- too young to put out in the barn. Besides, it was fall, and the nights were getting cold. We would have to keep them in the house until they were older. But Grandpa didn't like having animals inside the house. Where would we put them?

When Michelle brought the kittens home that evening, I was stunned. I took one look at them and said, "MICHELLE! These *ARE* Siamese cats!" AUGH!!

I told Michelle she would have to keep them in her room and keep the door shut *all* the time. We hoped Grandpa Roger wouldn't find out about them until they were old enough to go to the barn.

Nigel, the bigger of the Siamese kittens, was long, sleek-coated, and slender. That was the one Michelle had picked out. The more petite kitten was cute, but not as beautiful as Nigel.

Years ago, your Great Grandpa Harry and Great Grandma Gwen had a cat they named Itty Bitty because she was so tiny. I always thought that was a cute name, so I called the more petite Siamese kitten Itty Bitty.

We managed to keep the kittens hidden in Michelle's room for a few weeks without Grandpa Roger knowing they were there. I don't remember how he found out about them, but he did. Maybe he heard them meowing. Or, perhaps he smelled their litter box. Grandpa has an excellent nose for smelling!

Needless to say, he was *not* happy. He insisted they be put outside immediately. I tried to convince him they were too young to fend for themselves, and it wouldn't be safe to put them outside. He was not giving in. "They cannot stay in the house," he said very sternly. Sadly, Michelle and I put them outside.

The following day we went outside to look for the kittens. We noticed a stretch of grass missing from the front yard. It looked like someone must have skid their bicycle tire on the grass. We called "Here kitty, kitty! Here kitty, kitty! No kitties came running.

Grandpa Roger happened to be outside when we were calling them. "Can't find them?" he asked. I said, "No."

"Well, they have to be around somewhere," he said as he started looking for them. Then, he saw the dirt patch in the yard. "Oh, no," he said as he covered his eyes with his hands. "What?" I asked.

Seeming very upset, he told us he remembered seeing a coyote in our front yard the night before. The coyote grabbed something in its mouth and quickly ran away. Grandpa didn't think anything about it at the time. But now, as he saw the patch of grass missing, he told us that was exactly where he saw the coyote skid into the yard. We all knew at that moment what had probably happened. One of the kittens was the coyote's dinner that night.

Grandpa Roger felt *horrible!* He was the one who insisted on putting the kittens out, and now, at least one of them was missing. The three of us quickly started looking all around Too Little Ranch for any sign of a kitten.

I headed for the backyard. I looked everywhere I could think of: under the deck, in the bushes, in the flowers, near the swing set. But no kitty. I walked over to the woodpile. And then I heard it--- a soft "meow." There, in the very middle of the woodpile, was little Itty Bitty. She was so scared. I picked her up and hugged her close to me.

Grandpa Roger felt so bad that he had insisted on us putting the kittens outside. He felt even worse because Michelle's kitty, Nigel, did not survive the night. Still, it surprised both Michelle and me when Grandpa told us that Itty Bitty could now stay in the house.

After Monica and Michelle grew up and left home, I started adopting feral cats from the Humane Society. A feral cat is a cat who has either never had any contact with humans or her contact with humans has lessened over time. She is fearful of people and survives on her own outdoors. These are perfect cats to have on a farm. I adopted four of them in a matter of two years. At least they lived outdoors!

Michelle was responsible for bringing home most of our cats. I have to admit, though, that I brought home my fair share as well!

And Grandpa Roger said,

"No More Animals!"

Grace Newcomb

CHAPTER SIX

HORSES

This chapter is about our horses. There were only two, and believe it or not, Grandpa Roger favored getting both of them! Little One, our first horse, wasn't little at all! We needed a step ladder to get on her! She was a gentle giant, though, just the right horse for Michelle. Yes, nine-year-old Michelle is the one who wanted a horse. Does that surprise you? She took riding lessons and participated in 4-H with Little One. Little One, a funny name for such a big horse.

Monica rode Little One a few times, but riding was not her passion. I rode Little One as often as Michelle did. Grandpa Roger rode Little One a couple of times also. The last time he rode her was when the saddle shifted and slipped down under her belly. Grandpa fell off! He watched Little One continue to trot down the hill, saddle dangling, as he sat on the ground. She stopped at the bottom of the hill. She turned around and looked back at Grandpa as if to say, "What are you doing up there?"

Grandpa Roger and I built the barn from the first corner post to the roof. We did host a work party one Saturday and invited his siblings and your Great Grandpa Harry to come help do some of the heavier work. When the day was done, we fed them a good meal.

I loved that barn. Sliding the two big barn doors open, you walked into the center aisle that extended to the back end of the barn. On the left, there were stacks of hay bales. Beyond the hay bales was a horse stall.

To the right of the aisle was the tack room. That's where we kept saddles, bridles, reins, grooming equipment, horse blankets, fly masks, and anything else we might need for the horses. Horse tack is expensive. That's why that room had a door, so we could lock it if someone tried to steal the tack. Beyond the tack room was another horse stall.

The center aisle was used to saddle up the horses or groom them. The back of the barn was open to the fenced pasture.

Since I had always wanted a horse, Grandpa decided it was okay if we bought one for me, too. So a year or so after we purchased Little One, we bought Many Moons.

It's a good thing he wasn't our first horse. When we went to look at him, he was very calm. I rode him around the arena to see how he responded to direction. He seemed fine to us, so we bought him.

What we didn't know is that the owners had given him some medication to make him very calm. We had heard that people sometimes did this to sell an animal, but we didn't have enough horse experience to know that's what these people had done.

By the time we got him home, the medication had worn off, and he was one scared horse! He reared up when we tried to put the saddle on him. He jerked his head up and away from us when we put our hand anywhere near his head. Once we got the saddle on him, Michelle carefully put her foot in the stirrup and hoisted herself up onto the saddle. He immediately reared up, causing her to fall off his back. We hadn't even walked him out of the aisle yet!

God protected Michelle that day. She didn't get hurt. Because he was so fearful of human touch, we think he had been mistreated sometime during his life. It was definitely a learning experience for us.

We decided that Many Moons needed a new name: one that fit his personality. Whenever we took him on a trail ride, he nibbled on the bushes alongside the trail every chance he got. So we renamed him Mr. Nibbles.

It took a couple of years for Mr. Nibbles to completely trust us. We treated him very gently and talked softly and calmly to him. Over time, he learned we were not going to hurt him.

We still had to be cautious when we put a saddle on him, especially when we tightened up the cinch. The cinch is the strap that runs under his belly to connect to the other side of the saddle. That's what keeps the saddle from falling off the horse.

Because we were so gentle with him, he learned our hands were safe, and he eventually let us touch and pet his head without jerking away. It made me feel so good to have gained Mr. Nibbles' trust. He even learned to accept carrots from my piano students.

Horses are expensive pets to own. I did not ask Grandpa for any more horses.

CHAPTER SEVEN

THE FEED STORE

Over the years I brought home a variety of animals. Among them were two parakeets (Cheep and Chirp), four goldfish (Goldie, Finley, Forrest, and Jennie), and four rabbits (Shady, Lassie, Lucy, and Ricky). Naturally, I bought two girls and two boy rabbits so that when they were old enough, they would produce baby rabbits: more animals for Too Little Ranch!

Feed stores, where you buy hay and other supplies for farm animals, also have different types of animals for sale, like rabbits, baby chicks, and ducklings.

As a child, I fondly remember going to the feed store in Kent, Washington, where I lived, with your Great Grandpa Harry. I loved going there with him. I'm not really sure why I enjoyed it so much. Maybe it was the smell of the hay. Or perhaps it was the old wood floor in the feed store. I can still see those worn, rugged boards in my mind. Maybe it was because the feed store was near the railroad tracks, and we'd often see trains go by when we were there. Or perhaps I just liked being with my Dad. At any rate, feed stores are one of my favorite places.

One sunny spring morning, I drove to the Graham Hay Market to buy pet food. I think the only animals we had at the time were Mr. Nibbles, RT, and Slinky. Often in the spring, feed stores have baby chicks for sale. Sure enough, right at the front of the store were two water troughs.

It's common to raise chicks and ducklings in an old water trough. The sides of the trough are tall enough that the birds can't hop out. The bottom of the water trough is covered with sawdust shavings. That makes a soft bed for the babies. A heat lamp is usually hung above the trough to keep the babies warm. One trough had chicks in it, and the other had cute little ducklings.

By now, you know how hard it is for me to resist bringing home cute little baby animals! I walked past the ducklings. Then I turned around and bent down to check them out. I was there to buy hay for Mr. Nibbles. That was it. Just hay. I walked away.

I placed my hay order with the clerk. She called someone on her Walkie Talkie to tell him she needed two bales of hay brought to the front of the store. I waited inside the store for the young man to get the hay.

While I waited I watched the ducklings. We still had Little One's old water trough in the barn. We also had a massive pile of wood shavings that we used for Mr. Nibbles' horse stall. Hmmm... We already had a heat lamp in the tack room to keep Slinky warm in the winter. I guess the only other things I would need would be a water feeder and duck food.

As I stepped up to the counter to pay for the hay, I said, "I'll take a water feeder, a bag of duck food...and two ducklings, please."

Yep. I did it. I bought two *cute* ducklings!

CHAPTER EIGHT

THE TACK ROOM

With hay loaded in the back of the truck and two ducklings, duck food, and a water feeder on the seat beside me, I headed home.

As I drove home, I began to think. "Uh-oh, Grandpa Roger is *not* going to be happy with me bringing home two more animals."

I convinced myself that my purchases were okay. Besides, I would have been very embarrassed if I returned the ducklings within minutes of buying them.

You'd think I would have learned my lesson about bringing more animals home after the RT incident. But no. My love of animals outweighed my common sense. Now I had to figure out how to hide them from Grandpa.

The perfect place for the ducklings was inside the tack room. Little One's old water trough was already in there. I put sawdust shavings in the bottom of the trough, filled the water feeder with water, and put their food in a feeder we already had. I hung a heat lamp over the top of the trough to keep them warm. Then I gently put the two ducklings in the water trough and closed the tack room door.

Every morning and every evening, I went to the barn to feed Mr. Nibbles. Nothing unusual. But now it took me a little longer because I fed and watered the ducklings, too.

All was well until three weeks later when Grandpa Roger went to the barn looking for a shovel.

As he opened the two sliding barn doors, he noticed the door to the tack room was closed. "Hmmm, that's strange," he thought. "That door is usually open. I wonder why it's closed."

He heard a noise but wasn't quite sure what it was. As he walked toward the door, the noise became louder. *Cheep, cheep, cheep! Cheep, cheep, cheep!* He opened the tack room door.

"*OH NO!* She's done it again!" he said as he covered his eyes with one hand. Then he shook his head and chuckled to himself. Grandpa walked back to the house where I was busy making lunch.

"So, dear… how long have you had those ducks in the tack room?"

"Ducks? Hmmm? *Ohhhh*, you mean those two little duck-lings in the water trough?"

"Yes, dear, those two little ducklings in the water trough in the tack room."

I looked guilty. "Mmmmm---about three weeks," I said sheepishly. "What took you so long to notice?" We both started laughing and gave each other a big hug.

"Have you named them yet?" Grandpa asked.

"No, but I think they are very lucky ducks to be here at Too Little Ranch. How about Lucky Ducky and Lucy Goosey?"

Grandpa thought the whole thing was pretty funny, but he still told me,

"No More Animals!"

Grace Newcomb

CHAPTER NINE

FREE DUCKS

Lucky Ducky and Lucy Goosey soon outgrew the water trough. It was time to let them freely waddle around the barn and pasture. Waddle, waddle, waddle---they *sure* did waddle. AND---poop, poop, poop! They pooped even more than they waddled! They pooped *everywhere*! Even in the center aisle of the barn where we walked!

Of all the animals we had at Too Little Ranch, the ducks were by far the messiest.

There wasn't a spot in the barn or pasture where they hadn't pooped. It was stinky, too! After a year of scraping poop off the bottom of my boots every day, I was *done* with ducks!

I made a cardboard sign that read FREE DUCKS and placed it at the end of our driveway by the mailbox. Within an hour, a small truck with a canopy on the back drove into our driveway. A short, thin man got out of the truck and asked in broken English, "You have free ducks?"

"Yes, I do. They're out here in the pasture. If you want them, you'll have to catch them yourself," I told the man. I was not about to run around the pasture chasing ducks that didn't want to be caught. I have to admit, though, it *was* sort of funny watching the man do just that!

One at a time, he loaded the ducks into the back of his truck. He closed the canopy door, thanked me, and drove away. As I watched the truck leave the driveway, Lucky and Lucy were pecking at the canopy window as if to say, "Hey, let us out! Let us out!"

Watching my ducks peck at the window tugged at my heartstrings. Then it dawned on me…Lucky Ducky and Lucy Goosey were probably not going to be the man's pets. Instead, they would be his family's dinner. I felt awful. It was too late to do anything about it. The truck was already gone.

Grace Newcomb

CHAPTER TEN

ARPEGGIOS

One afternoon while teaching Sarah, one of my piano students, she noticed that I seemed sad.

"Why are you so sad, Mrs. C?" she asked.

With tears in my eyes, I told Sarah that RT had died. Sarah owned a dog, too, so she understood how hard it was for me to say goodbye to RT. Wiping the tears from my eyes and wanting to change the subject, I said, "Well, let's get back to your piano lesson, Sarah."

"Most musical terms are Italian. Today we are going to learn to play arpeggios. It's spelled a-r-p-e-g-g-i-o, and we say 'aar-**PEH**-jee-oh.' 'Arpeggio' means 'broken chord'."

"You already know that a chord is playing two or more keys at the same time. When we play arpeggios we play these three keys one at a time, like this."

I showed Sarah how to play an arpeggio. "Now you try," I said. Sarah played the arpeggio quickly and easily.

"By Jove! I think you've got it!" My British accent always made her laugh. Her laughter was just the thing I needed to cheer me up.

Continuing on, I pointed to the word arpeggio on the page of music. Sarah blurted out, "It looks like aar-**PEGGY**-oh!"

Chuckling, I replied, "Yes, it does, Sarah, but we pronounce it the Italian way by saying aar-**peh**-jee-oh."

Sarah quickly reminded me that she was in advanced classes at school. "I'm really good at reading and sounding out new words. It should be aar-**PEGGY**-oh."

"Yes, yes, it does look like that. However, Sarah, the proper way to pronounce it in Italian is aar-**peh**-jee-oh."

It was quiet for an awkward moment. I could tell Sarah was thinking. "Hey, I know! You should name your next dog Peggy, for aar-**PEGGY**-ohs, because you're a piano teacher!"

I couldn't help laughing at her suggestion. "That's a great idea, Sarah! I think I'll do that!"

Grace Newcomb

CHAPTER ELEVEN

CAMPING

It was seven long years before any more animals came to live at Too Little Ranch. In fact, by that time, all we had were cats; Itty Bitty (the indoor kitty) and Mr. Slinky (our barn cat). I would have loved to get another dog, but Grandpa Roger said it would have to stay outside.

I stubbornly said, "Okay, I guess we won't get one then, because I want a dog that can live in the house with us."

So, in a way, we had come to an agreement. However, it was not an agreement that made me happy.

One summer during those seven years, Grandpa and I went camping in Oregon. As usual, we stopped to talk with other campers as we leisurely strolled through the campground.

This particular night, we stopped to talk to a lovely older couple who had a big dog. As we stepped onto their campsite, the friendly dog eagerly greeted us. His tail was wagging a hundred miles an hour (not really, but it was wagging fast!) as he rubbed up against Grandpa's legs, begging to be petted. We were both so impressed with the friendliness of their dog that I started asking questions.

"What breed of dog is he? Does he shed? Where did you get him? Are they all this friendly?"

The friendly couple told us the dog was a mix between a golden retriever and a poodle. This combination is called a Goldendoodle. Most of them don't shed, but some do. They bought him in Canada. And yes, Goldendoodles are known for being people-friendly dogs.

As we walked back to our camper, I told Grandpa Roger, "I know the kind of dog I want next." He made no comment, and that was the end of that conversation!

CHAPTER TWELVE

MICHELLE TO THE RESCUE

Another year went by. We still only had Itty Bitty and Mr. Slinky. I was getting sadder and sadder each day. Grandpa and I were talking about my sadness one evening, and he said, "I've changed my mind."

"Changed your mind about what," I asked.

"About getting a dog," he replied.

I couldn't believe what I was hearing. I questioned Grandpa, "Are you serious?"

Quietly and calmly, he responded, "Yes."

Still not sure he would commit to letting a dog live in the house, I asked, "And it can live in the house with us?"

"Yes, I think it will be good for you," he said, looking me straight in the eyes.

I burst into happy tears, jumped onto his lap, and gave him a great big hug. "Oh, thank you, honey," I said as I wiped the tears from my eyes.

That was an extraordinary moment I will cherish forever; because once Grandpa makes up his mind about something, he doesn't usually change it.

It wasn't until a week later that I found out Michelle and Grandpa Roger had been talking about how to help me overcome my sadness. Michelle had suggested that perhaps he should rethink his firm "No" about getting a dog. He took her advice, reconsidered, and changed his mind.

I wasted no time googling Goldendoodles. Were there any in the United States? Were there any in Washington? Who sold them? Are the dogs health-tested to make sure they don't have any severe health problems?

After days and days of researching, I came across the 4E Kennels website. They specialized in breeding Goldendoodles. After chatting with the owner and getting answers to all my questions, I made my decision. I would buy a female Goldendoodle from 4E Kennels in Pahrump, Nevada.

I already knew what I was going to name her. That was easy! Her name would be Peggy, for aar-**PEGGY**-ohs, because I was a piano teacher!

TM

CHAPTER THIRTEEN

PEGGY

Buying a dog from a professional dog breeder was a whole new experience for me. I learned a lot in the process.

One of the things I didn't know was that breeders actually have unique names for each litter born. So, for instance, a litter might be named the Disney Litter. The puppies then would be called Disney characters, like Mickey Mouse, Cinderella, etc.

When "Peggy" was born, her litter name was the Medieval Mighties. The puppies were named for places and people that existed between 1400 and 1500 (the Medieval Age). There was Viking, Romeo, Margaret, Eleanor, Constantinople, Knight, Castle, and Royal.

The breeder regularly posted pictures of the growing puppies on her website. I eagerly watched for new photos every day. In my opinion, all of the puppies were cute except one--Eleanor. I thought her head was too big for her body. I remember saying to myself, "That's the *last puppy* I would choose."

This breeder, Jeanette Forrey, had created her own puppy evaluation process to ensure her clients get the right dog for them, and that the puppy's needs are honored.

When the puppies are seven weeks old, Jeanette does the puppy evaluation. She sets up a small fenced area with various toys and objects in it. One at a time, each puppy is placed inside the fencing. One person is in the fenced area, too, interacting with the puppy. The evaluator watches the person and the puppy play together. Some puppies prefer toys over humans. Other puppies love to chase balls. Then some just like to lie around and not do much of anything.

I knew I wanted a puppy that loved humans more than anything else. After all the evaluations were completed, guess which puppy was found to be the one that loved humans the most? You guessed it-—Eleanor!

Grace Newcomb

CHAPTER FOURTEEN

ELEANOR

I trusted Jeanette's puppy evaluation and flew to Pahrump, Nevada, to pick up Eleanor. Since I had followed her journey from birth as Eleanor, I had bonded with her and that name.

I tried to call her Peggy, but it just didn't fit. She was an 'Eleanor,' not a 'Peggy.' So, Eleanor, she was, and Eleanor she still is today. Although, I usually call her Ellie.

One of my piano student families called her Ellie Mae. They said 'Eleanor' was too elegant of a name because she was such an active, rambunctious puppy!

When Ellie turned six months old, I told Grandpa Roger I thought she needed a sister to play with. (Ha, ha, ha—did you see that coming?)

She needed a lot of exercise to keep her happy and out of trouble. Once a week, I would take her to doggy daycare to play with other dogs. It was so good for her—and for me! I needed a break from her if I wanted to get anything else done!

You can probably guess what Grandpa's answer was to my request for another dog. I tried really hard to convince him to reconsider.

I even thought of starting my own dog breeding business. That was a HUGE "NO!"

We were getting close to retiring from our jobs and Grandpa wanted to travel in retirement. He said our camper was barely big enough for us and one dog, let alone two. That was true!

The next thing I knew, Grandpa started looking to buy a motorhome. They are much larger than a camper and would be more comfortable for traveling.

After a year of searching, he finally found what he was looking for at the right price. I could hardly believe my eyes when I saw it! It was so big and beautiful. I never thought in my wildest dreams we would own anything that nice.

Grandpa Roger told everyone that he *had* to buy it because now we had Eleanor, and she wouldn't fit in the camper. I have to agree, the motorhome is much more spacious and comfortable for the three of us.

CHAPTER FIFTEEN

RETIRED

In 2017, we decided it was time to retire. Slinky had passed away, so the only animals we had were Itty Bitty and Eleanor.

Grandpa did not want to travel with a cat in the motorhome because cat litter boxes can be messy and stinky. It made me extremely sad (and yes, I cried…a lot) the day we gave Itty Bitty to a man that Grandpa worked with. I have to believe Itty Bitty is living her best life with him.

We sold Too Little Ranch and started traveling south to warmer weather and sunshine. It was Grandpa Roger, me, and Eleanor in the motorhome. Now we were *really* living Too Little Ranch style! In fact, there was no ranch at all! No room for any more animals.

After living in the Pacific Northwest, where the weather is cloudy most days, we wanted to live in a place with warm weather and lots of sunshine.

After researching the weather statistics of several cities in the United States, we decided to relocate to Yuma, Arizona, where the sun shines 308 days a year. Many people spend the winter months there and leave during the summer when temperatures are 105 degrees and hotter. Grandpa Roger said he'd like to do that.

On our way to Yuma, we stopped in Pahrump, Nevada, to visit friends. It's interesting how God works sometimes. We had no intention of living in Pahrump. But God's plan for us unfolded right before our eyes, and we followed His leading. We bought a house, and as you know, we now live in Pahrump!

Do you remember who lived in Pahrump at 4E Kennels for the first eight weeks of her life? If you said Eleanor, you're right!

Guess where Grandma Carol started volunteering? Yep! 4E Kennels, where there are *lots of Goldendoodles!*

Oh, dear! So many adorable puppies. So tempting!

As you already know, I eventually brought home another Goldendoodle, Miss Reba. I named her Reba because her fur is red, I like Reba McEntire, and her Grandmother's name was Reba!

4E Kennels is on a 5-acre farm. Besides dogs, there are goats, peacocks, cats, chickens, deer, and horses.

The Mama chickens had baby chickens. And then those chickens had more chickens! 4E Kennels ended up with way too many chickens! The owners asked me if I would like to take a couple of baby chicks home.

Uh-Oh...are you thinking what I'm thinking?

Will Grandma Carol bring home another animal?

Will Grandpa Roger once again say,

"No More Animals"? What do you think?

ARPEGGIO PEGGY

(Chorus)
Her Mom was a Golden Retriever.
Her Dad was a curly-haired Poodle.
You put the two together and what do you get?
Golden. Doodle.
Doodle Do Doot!

(Verse One)
Arpeggio Peggy is my Goldendoodle.
She's from 4E Kennels in Pahrump, Nevada.
I bet you wonder how she got her name.
Glad you asked, I'll gladly tell ya.

I was teaching Sarah to play arpeggios.
She is very verbal, you know.
It's spelled a-r-p-e-g-g-i-o and we say, "aar-**peh**-jee-oh"

She said, "Oh, no, no, no. It doesn't look like that!
It looks like it should be "aar-**peggy**-oh**."**
I said, "Yes, yes it does.
But two G's in Italian can sometimes sound like '**Juh**,' not
'**Guh**.'

She said, "I like **Guh**."
I said, **"It. Is. Juh!"**

Then quick-witted Sarah came back with a reply…
"Hey! I know! You should name your next dog Peggy, for
aar-**peggy**-ohs, because you're a piano teacher!

(Chorus)
Her Mom was a Golden Retriever.
Her Dad was a curly-haired Poodle.
You put the two together and what do you get?
Golden. Doodle.
Doodle Do Doot!

(Verse Two)
Now Arpeggio Peggy is NOT my Goldendoodle.
Still from 4E Kennels in Pahrump, Nevada.
But there's just one thing I forgot to tell ya.

She was born into Grace and Watson's Medieval Mighty Litter.
And Jeanette already named her…
Eleanor!
Doodle Do Doot!
Pahrump!

Copyright 2016

For sheet music and recording,
please email carolchampney@gmail.com

ABOUT THE AUTHOR

C arol Champney began her writing career at the age of thirteen. Writing letters to her best friend every day for eight years laid the groundwork for her love of writing.

She loves animals, being creative, taking pictures of old barns, teaching and making music, and of course, writing.

Carol Champney is the Award-Winning author of Too Little Ranch. The "*Finally Finishing Her First Book Award*" was presented to her in July 2021 by none other than—-Grandma Carol!

It's a Best-Seller, too!

(According to Grandma Carol, that is!)

CPSIA information can be obtained
at www.ICGtesting.com
Printed in the USA
LVHW021056110422
715872LV00004B/246